WOOD

CRAFT PROJECTS

Graham Carrick

Illustrated by
Malcolm S. Walker

Rourke Enterprises, Inc.
Vero Beach, FL 32964

Craft Projects

CLAY
FABRICS AND YARNS
NATURAL MATERIALS
PAPER
SCRAP MATERIALS
WOOD

First published in the
United States in 1990 by
Rourke Enterprises, Inc.
Vero Beach, FL 32964

Text © 1990 Rourke Enterprises, Inc.

Library of Congress Cataloging-in-Publication Data

Carrick, Graham, 1947-
   Wood / by Graham Carrick.
    p. cm. -- (Craft projects)
   Bibliography : p.
   Includes index
   Summary: Details how to make a variety of projects by
constructing and carving wood.
   ISBN 0-86592-484-8
   1. Woodwork -- Juvenile literature. (1. Woodwork.
2. Handicraft.)
I. Title. II. Series.
TT185.C37 1990
684' . 08 -- dc20   89 - 32739
                                                    CIP
                                                    AC

© Copyright Wayland (Publishers) Ltd.
61 Western Road, Hove, East Sussex BN3 1JD, England.

Printed in Italy by G. Canale and C. S. p. A., Turin

WOOD
Contents

Introduction

Here is a list of useful materials you could collect to make the projects.

Wood strips ¼" x 1¼" and larger (Balsa strips are available in hobby stores.)
Pre-planed scraps of softwood
Dowels: all sizes
Used matchsticks
Wooden chopsticks
Toothpicks
Ice cream sticks

Projects in wood need not be expensive. Scraps of wood can usually be bought from lumberyards, and small pieces are sometimes even available at no charge. Also, you can make many interesting things without having to buy many tools.

Working with wood involves both constructing and carving. You can construct by joining pieces of wood together with glue and carve by removing pieces of wood with a saw and a file.

The projects suggested here will introduce you to working with wood in a variety of ways. Once you start to make something, you will have ideas of your own. Enjoy exploring these ideas and have fun with the projects.

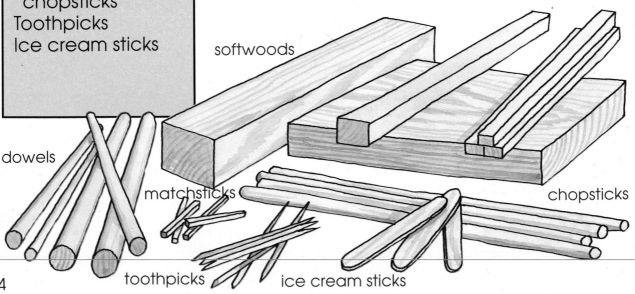

softwoods

dowels

matchsticks

chopsticks

toothpicks

ice cream sticks

Materials

There are many kinds of wood. Examine pieces for differences in color, hardness, pattern and smell.

The striped pattern in wood is called the grain and is made up of small fibers or particles. A knot is an eye shape caused by a branch. Woods are grouped as **hardwoods** and **softwoods**. Softwoods are easier to work with than hardwoods because they are soft and have a straight grain. Pine is the most common softwood; oak and maple are typical hardwoods.

There are a number of boards made from wood that are useful where you need broad strips of material.

Blockboard consists of strips of softwood glued together and sandwiched between thin layers of wood called veneers. Its strength makes it useful as a base for your work.

Particleboard is a strong material made from wood chips and resin, and is also useful as a base.

Hardboard comes in a variety of strengths. It is made from waste wood and resin. It can be easily cut and drilled and will prove useful in many of the projects.

Plywood is made from veneers that are glued together so that the grains in alternate layers run in opposite directions. Plywood made of birch veneers is the easiest to saw. Splintering is best avoided by sticking masking tape or Scotch tape along the line to be sawed.

blockboard

particleboard

hardboard
smooth side
↓
rough side

1

2

3

plywood
(3-ply)

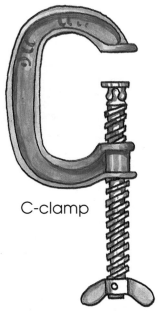

C-clamp

You will need a bench or a table that's a comfortable height. It is safer to work at a surface that is a little too low than at one that is too high. If you are using a table, protect the top from damage by attaching a piece of board with C-clamps. Ask an adult to help you.

C-clamps can also be used to secure work to your bench or table, or to hold glued parts together until set. It is helpful to have C-clamps in a variety of sizes ranging from 3" to 6".

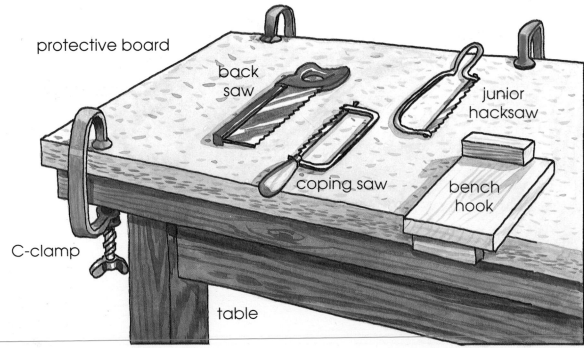

protective board

back saw

junior hacksaw

coping saw

bench hook

C-clamp

table

Here is a list of other equipment you will need to make the projects.

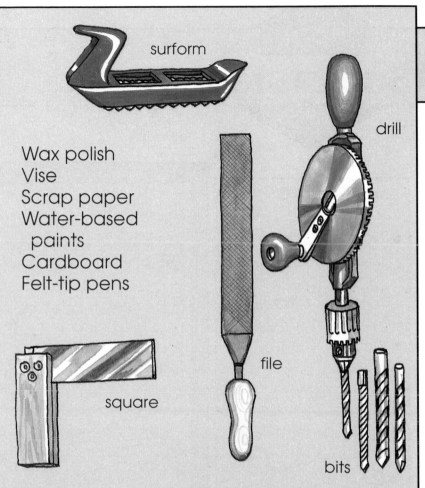
surform

drill

Bench hook or
  sawing board
Back saw (8")
Coping saw
Junior hacksaw
Surform tools
Files
Hand drill and
  twist bits
Sandpaper in a
  variety of grades
  from coarse
  to fine
Try square
Pencil and ruler
Carpenter's wood
  glue

Wax polish
Vise
Scrap paper
Water-based
  paints
Cardboard
Felt-tip pens

square

file

bits

Safety

Saws can be dangerous if used incorrectly. Follow these rules:

1. Secure the wood to your workbench with a vise, C-clamp or bench hook.
2. Saw away from your body.
3. Keep your fingers well away from the cutting edge of the saw.

Handle all tools very carefully. If in doubt about any of the projects ask an adult to help you.

point index
finger forward
against
handle

saw at a
slight angle to
the surface of the wood

Sculpture in wood

You will need

- Scraps of pre-planed softwood of suitable sizes for your chosen subject
- Pencil
- Vise
- Coping saw
- Surform tools (one surform with flat blade, one with curved blade and another with round blade) or rasp
- Files (half-round file and round file)
- Sandpaper
- Wood glue

- Varnish or polyurethane

1. Decide what you are going to make. Will it be a duck, squirrel, cat, apple, or something else? Study its shape by looking either at the real thing or at drawings and photographs. If possible, study the subject from a number of viewpoints - front, back, top and one or both sides.

2. Choose a block of wood for each major part of your subject. Use a pencil to outline the shapes of these parts. Draw straight lines where parts are to be joined.

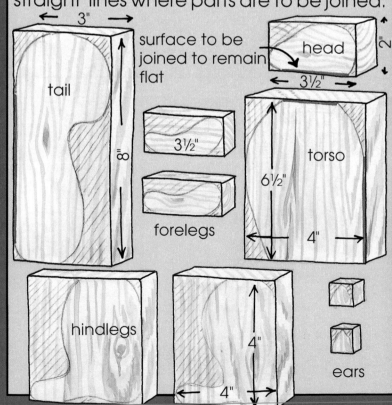

surface to be joined to remain flat

3"

tail

8"

head

2"

3½"

3½"

torso

6½"

4"

forelegs

hindlegs

4"

4"

ears

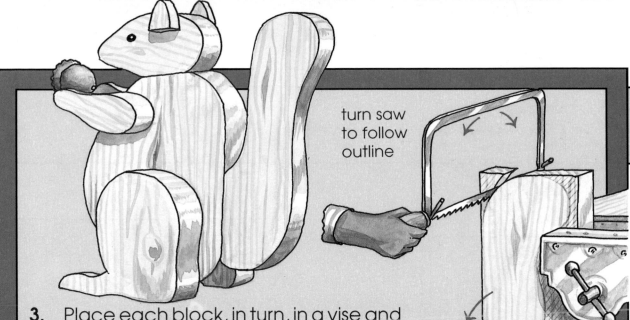

turn saw
to follow
outline

turn wood to
continue sawing
downward

3. Place each block, in turn, in a vise and cut around the outline with a coping saw. The block should be turned as necessary so that you are aiming down throughout your sawing.

Instead of cutting cleanly like scissors, saws remove wood as sawdust. Therefore, you should saw not on the outline but on the outside of it. Otherwise your work will end up smaller than planned.

Where you need to saw along the grain, do this slowly and gently, to avoid splitting the wood. If your wood does split, repair it with glue.

4. When you have cut around all the outlines, round off each part by shaping with surforms, rasps and files. But remember that surfaces to be joined should be kept flat. Grip the surform or file at both ends and pull it forwards and backwards across the wood.

5. Smooth each part with sandpaper.

6. Join the parts together with wood glue.

7. If you want your sculpture to have a glossy finish, apply several coats of varnish or polyurethane.

More ideas

You may not have scraps of softwood of suitable sizes for carving. This can be overcome by joining strips of wood together with glue (for example, ½" x ½", or ½" x 1"). Wipe away excess glue with a dry cloth. When the glue has dried, the blocks you have made may be carved in the same way as above.

Collage in wood

You will need

- Paper on which to draw your plan
- Piece of blockboard, particleboard, hardboard or plywood for your background
- Scraps of hardboard, plywood and softwood
- Matchsticks and ice cream sticks
- Vise
- Coping saw (and back saw if cutting straight through thicker strips of wood)
- Sandpaper
- Wood glue
- Water-based paints

A collage picture or design is "in relief." That means that it projects out from a flat surface. The greater the thickness of the materials that you use, the more they will stand out from the surface of your collage. Here is how to make a collage of a train.

1. Draw a plan of a train on paper. Make your drawing the actual size that you intend your collage to be.

2. Select pieces of hardboard, plywood and softwood for the parts of your picture. Choose pieces with different colors and grain patterns and of different thicknesses.

3. Draw outlines of the parts of your picture on the pieces of wood and board that you have chosen.

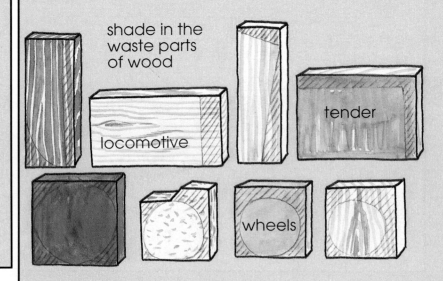

shade in the waste parts of wood

locomotive

tender

wheels

Outlines should be marked out from the edge, rather than the center of the wood or board. This avoids wastage of materials and saves you time in sawing.

4. Secure each piece, in turn, in a vise. Cut out the shape using a coping saw. Turn the wood in the vise, as necessary, so that you continue to saw downward. Saw on the waste side of your outline. Be extra careful when you need to saw along the grain, as this is where the wood may split.

5. Smooth each piece with sandpaper.

6. Arrange all the pieces you have cut out in their correct positions on the background board. Then stick them to the board with glue. Add detail to your collage with matchsticks and ice cream sticks, then decorate with paints.

More ideas

You can make a collage out of many things. Try combining materials with wood to make a picture of your school. You can use paper, twigs, cardboard, scraps of fabric, and many other things.

Building with wood scraps

You will need

- A collection of scraps of hardboard, plywood and softwood of different shapes and sizes. (Blockboard and particle-board are also useful provided they do not have to be cut.)
- Pencil, ruler and square

- Vise
- Coping saw (and back saw if cutting straight through thicker strips of wood)
- Sandpaper
- Wood glue

- Water-based paints

1. Decide what you would like to construct and study your scraps. What do they look like - a roof, a building?

2. Perhaps your scraps could be used to build a house. Draw lines on the wood to show where surplus wood needs to be removed. Where you need to draw a line at right angles to the edge of your wood, it is helpful to use a square.

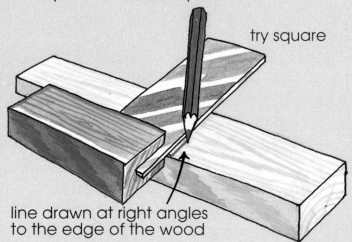

try square

line drawn at right angles to the edge of the wood

3. Shade in pencil on the waste side of the line.

4. Secure the wood in a vise. Saw along the waste side of the line, using a coping saw. (Use a back saw when cutting straight through thicker strips of wood.) Take extra care when sawing along the grain to prevent the wood from splitting.

5. Join the parts of your house with wood glue. (Or keep the parts separate as a ``construction kit'' toy for a young child.)

6. Decorate your house with water-based paints or by covering with all-purpose glue diluted with water (approximately two parts glue to one part water) to give it a glossy appearance. If you want your work to be colored and glossy, mix paint with diluted glue.

More ideas

Make some furniture for a doll's house.

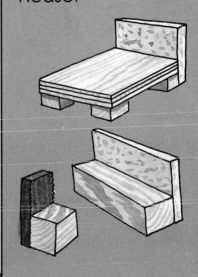

Making a frame

You will need

- Strips of wood ¼" to ½" square
- Cardboard and scissors
- Hardboard (where required to enclose the structure)
- Pencil and ruler
- Vise or bench hook
- Junior hacksaw or coping saw
- Sandpaper
- Wood glue
- Paints or felt-tip pens

This project will show you how to make a box shape that can be used as a basic framework for many things.

1. To make a strong, rectangular frame, first cut four strips of wood to the required length, using a junior hacksaw or coping saw. Before sawing, secure the wood in a vise. After sawing, smooth the ends of the wood with sandpaper.

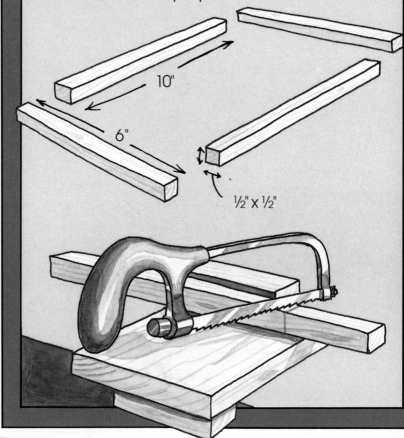

10"

6"

½" x ½"

2. Take a small sheet of cardboard (approximately 8" x 8"). Use your pencil and ruler to draw a grid of horizontal and vertical lines on the cardboard. Then draw diagonals in one direction only. You will end up with a network of triangles that can be cut out as needed.

3. Join the four strips of wood using wood glue. Then cut out four of the triangles from your cardboard. Glue the triangles to the corners of your frame. When the glue has dried, turn the frame over and glue four triangles to the other side in the same way.

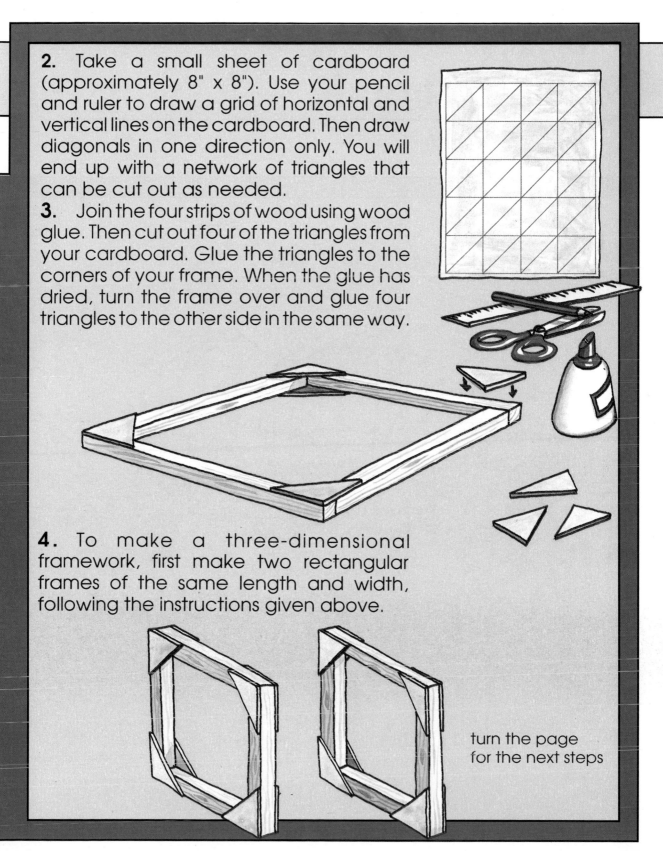

4. To make a three-dimensional framework, first make two rectangular frames of the same length and width, following the instructions given above.

turn the page
for the next steps

Making a frame

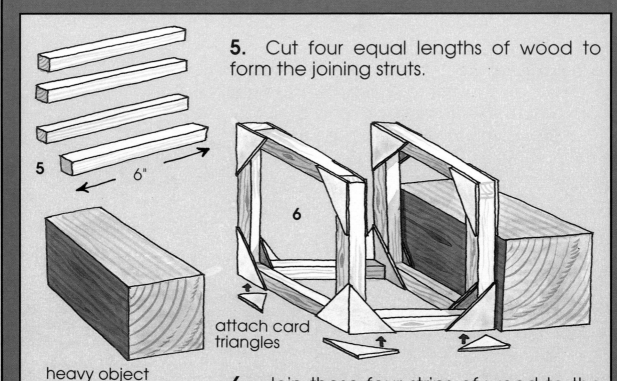

5. Cut four equal lengths of wood to form the joining struts.

5

6"

attach card triangles

heavy object to support uprights

6. Join these four strips of wood to the existing frames, using the card triangles that you have made. First join two strips at the base of the work. You will need eight card triangles - two for each corner. Glue the strips of wood to the existing frames. Then attach card triangles at each corner. If possible, get someone to help you by holding the upright frames in position while you attach the card triangles. Use two heavy objects to keep the existing frames in place until the glue has dried.

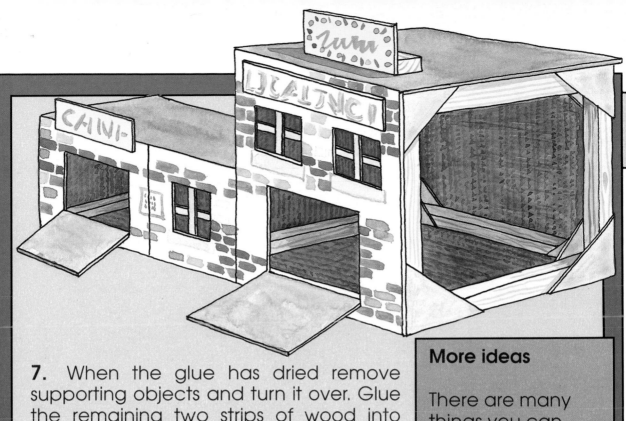

7. When the glue has dried remove supporting objects and turn it over. Glue the remaining two strips of wood into position, using eight more card triangles.

8. To this basic structure you can add further strips of wood as necessary, depending on what you wish to make.

9. You can cover and enclose your structure using cardboard or hardboard and decorate it with paints or felt-tip pens.

More ideas

There are many things you can make with wood strips. Why not try to make a farm scene with a farmhouse, a farmyard and maybe even some wooden animals and a tractor?

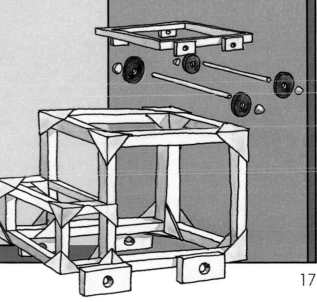

Bank

You will need

- ¼" to ½" wood strips approximately 60" in length
- Cardboard and scissors
- Hardboard (about 10" x 15")
- Pencil and ruler
- Try square
- Vise
- Junior hacksaw and coping saw
- Sandpaper
- Wood glue
- Water-based paints

Now that you know how to construct a frame, you can make a bank.

1. Use the technique shown on the previous pages to make the framework of your box.

2. Measure box before dividing hardboard into five pieces to cover framework. Use a try square to draw lines at right angles to the edge.

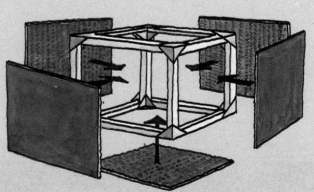

3. Cut out hardboard panels with a coping saw. Secure hardboard in a vise before sawing. Turn the hardboard, as necessary, so that you are able to saw downward throughout. Smooth the edges of hardboard panels with sandpaper.

4. Attach the base and side panels to the framework of your box, using glue.

5. Using a piece of cardboard, cut out the right size to cover the top of your box. Use pencil and ruler to draw a rectangular slot in the panel. The slot should be large enough to take a coin. Cut out the slot with scissors. First make a hole in the center of the slot with the point of your scissors. Insert the blade of the scissors into the hole and carefully cut around the outline.

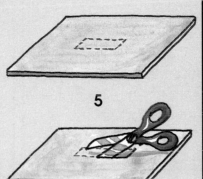

5

6. To get the lid to fit tightly, attach a frame or lip to the underside. Make this lip with strips of wood and attach with glue.

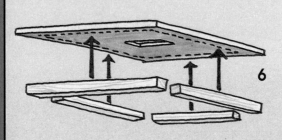

6

7

7. Cut a small piece of wood and glue it to the top of the lid as a handle.

8. You can decorate your box with water-based paints. For a glossy finish, mix paints with diluted glue.

More ideas

Make a box for your pens and pencils. Make a jewelry box.

Bird feeder

You will need

- A piece of plywood 18" x 18" (exterior quality wood will last longer out of doors)
- 60" length of ½" wood strip
- 8 brads or finish nails
- Bradawl or hand drill
- Hammer
- 1 yard of nylon cord
- Four metal screw eyes

You will need to find a suitable branch on a tree in your yard, or perhaps in the playground at school, for this bird feeder.

1. Using a junior hacksaw or coping saw, cut the wood into four lengths, two 18" and two 12" lengths, as shown below.

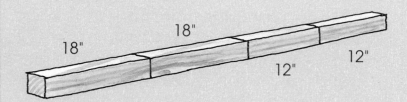

2. Using a bradawl or a hand drill, make two small holes for the nails in each piece of wood.

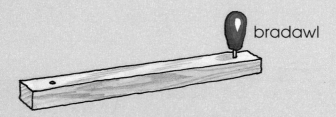

3. Hammer the nails through the wood before attaching to the plywood.

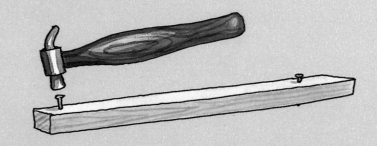

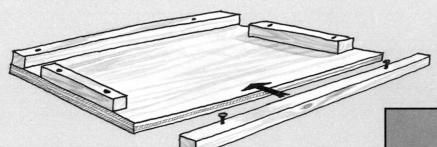

4. Attach the strips of wood to the plywood to make a rim. This will help prevent the food from being blown away.
5. Make holes for screw eyes on the ends of the bird feeder as shown below. Attach screw eyes and tie nylon cord to one side only. Loop cord over a suitable branch and fasten to the other side of the table.
6. Hang bags of nuts and fat from the screw eyes and put a plastic container of water on the feeder. Remember to change the water occasionally to keep it fresh.

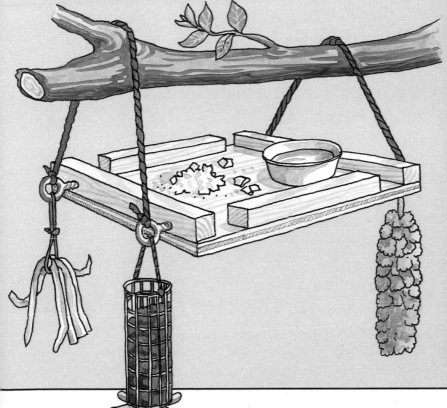

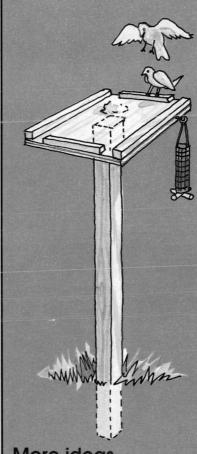

More ideas

Attach your bird feeder to an upright post. Make a study of the kinds of birds that visit your feeder.
Try different foods and see which the birds prefer.

Maze game

You will need

- Marble
- Piece of hardboard for the base of your maze
- Wood strips for the walls of your maze

- Paper, pencil and ruler
- Vise
- Coping saw
- Sandpaper
- Wood glue

1. Decide what shape and size you want for the base of your maze. Remember that it should be possible to work the maze easily with both hands.

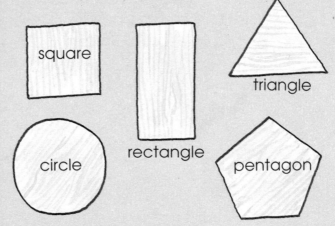

square

rectangle

triangle

circle

pentagon

2. Draw the shape of your game onto hardboard. Secure with a vise and cut out shape using a coping saw.

3. Draw possible designs for your maze. Make your drawings the actual size of the maze you intend to make. When plotting the passageways remember that the walls will be the thickness of your strips of wood and NOT the thickness of your pencil line. Your maze should include alternative routes, some of which are dead ends.

Decide where you want your starting point and finishing point to be. Copy the best design onto your baseboard.

start

finish

4. Using a coping saw, cut the strips of wood to form the walls of your maze. Before sawing, use a ruler to measure the length of wood that you need and use the pencil to mark where you need to cut. Secure the wood in a vise. When sawing is complete, smooth the ends of the wood with sandpaper. Place the walls of your maze in position on the baseboard, but do not glue them down yet.

Use a marble to test that the pathways of your maze are wide enough. The marble should be able to roll freely and not get stuck between walls. It should be possible for the marble to roll from start to finish.

5. Attach the walls to the baseboard with glue.

6. Decorate with water-based paints.

More ideas

Cover part of the maze with a roof of cardboard. The player must then navigate ``blind'' for part of the way.

You can bore small holes through particular positions on the base using a hand drill, then enlarge the holes with a round file to make traps for the marble.

Using a watch, you can time your family and friends to see who can get the marble from start to finish the fastest.

Pinball game

You will need

- Marble
- Piece of hardboard for the base of your game
- Wood scraps

- Paper, pencil and ruler
- Vise
- Coping saw or junior hacksaw
- Sandpaper
- Wood glue

- Water-based paints

1. Draw possible designs for a pinball game. Decide on the size and shape of your baseboard and whether or not you want a backboard for your game. What obstacles are to be placed on the board? What other features can your game have - bridges, slopes, tunnels and changes of level? How will the scoring work?

Goals may be placed almost anywhere on the baseboard. The lowest score should be given when the marble enters the easiest goal. The highest score should be given when the marble enters the most difficult goal.

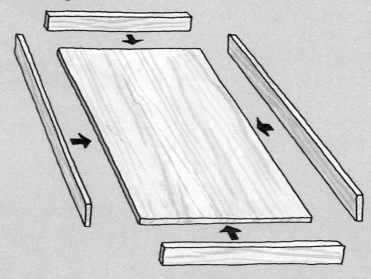

2. Cut your baseboard to the size and shape that you want. To saw hardboard you will need a vise and a coping saw.

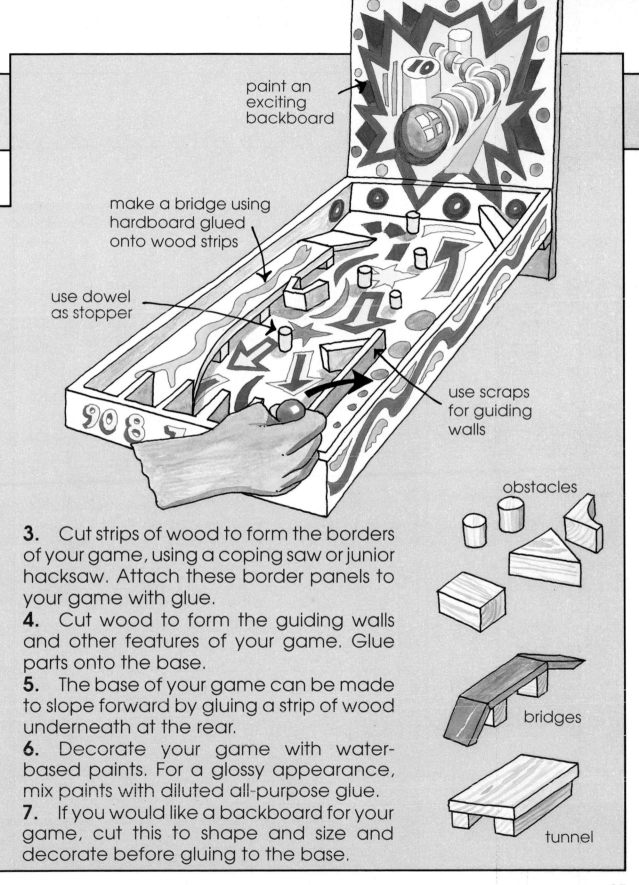

paint an exciting backboard

make a bridge using hardboard glued onto wood strips

use dowel as stopper

use scraps for guiding walls

obstacles

bridges

tunnel

3. Cut strips of wood to form the borders of your game, using a coping saw or junior hacksaw. Attach these border panels to your game with glue.

4. Cut wood to form the guiding walls and other features of your game. Glue parts onto the base.

5. The base of your game can be made to slope forward by gluing a strip of wood underneath at the rear.

6. Decorate your game with water-based paints. For a glossy appearance, mix paints with diluted all-purpose glue.

7. If you would like a backboard for your game, cut this to shape and size and decorate before gluing to the base.

Hoop game

You will need

- Hoops or rings of plastic, cardboard or wood
- Scraps of hardboard, plywood, or pre-planed softwood
- Round-headed nails 1¼" long or cup hooks
- Paper, pencil and ruler
- Vise
- Coping saw or junior hacksaw
- Sandpaper
- All-purpose glue
- Small hammer
- Water-based paints

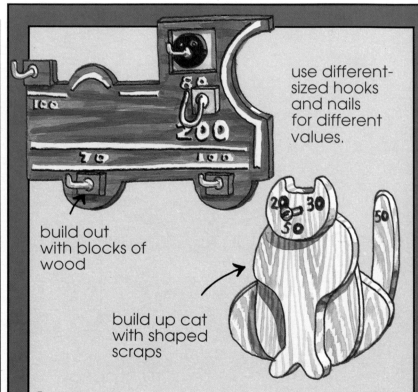

use different-sized hooks and nails for different values.

build out with blocks of wood

build up cat with shaped scraps

1. Decide what you are going to make - an animal, a building, a face, a vehicle, or a monster - then make some drawings of possible designs for your hoop game.

2. Choose suitable pieces of board and wood to make your game.

3. Cut them to shape and size using a coping saw or a junior hacksaw. Always draw the line to be cut on the wood and secure the wood in a vise before sawing.

4. Smooth the wood with sandpaper.

5. Glue the parts of the game together.

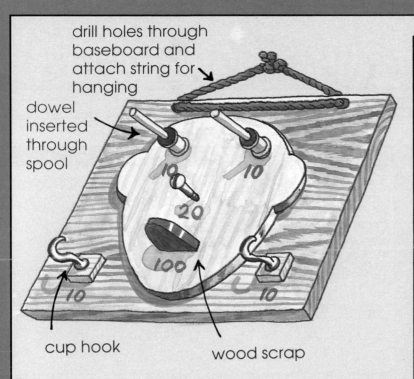

drill holes through baseboard and attach string for hanging

dowel inserted through spool

cup hook

wood scrap

More ideas

Make a hoop game in the shape of a figure, a robot for example.

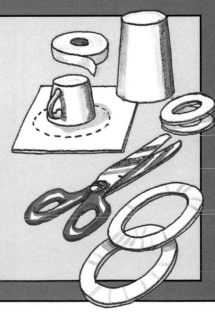

6. When the glue has dried, paint and decorate the game. For a glossy finish apply a coat of diluted glue.

7. Hammer the nails into place to use as targets.

Making rings from cardboard

Rings can be cut from cardboard with scissors. Draw around a circular object, like a coffee mug. Find a smaller circular object and make another circle inside the first circle. Cut out the ring with scissors. Strengthen and stiffen rings with tape. Stick tape over the ring and trim centers and edges on both sides.

Model adventure playground

You will need

- Piece of hard-board for the base of your game
- Scraps of wood
- Wood strips
- Dowels, used matchsticks, ice cream sticks
- Aluminum foil, spools and string
- Paper, cardboard, pencil, ruler and scissors
- Vise
- Coping saw or junior hacksaw
- Sandpaper
- Glue

1. If possible, visit an existing adventure playground. Which pieces of equipment seem to be the most popular? Why do you think this is?

Could any of the equipment be changed to provide greater interest or challenge, while still ensuring safety?

2. Make some drawings of possible designs for an adventure playground. You might like to give your playground a theme such as a ship or a castle.

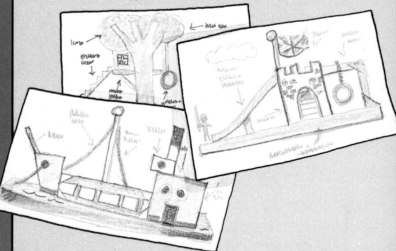

3. Select your best ideas for further development. Using techniques shown in previous sections, try to make your model adventure playground. Ask an adult to help you if you get stuck.

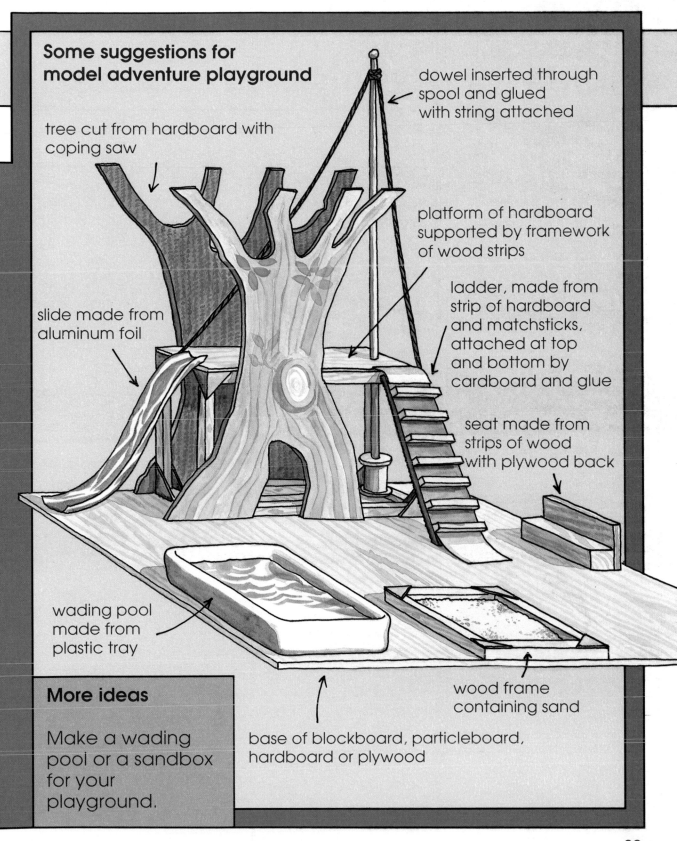

Some suggestions for model adventure playground

tree cut from hardboard with coping saw

dowel inserted through spool and glued with string attached

platform of hardboard supported by framework of wood strips

slide made from aluminum foil

ladder, made from strip of hardboard and matchsticks, attached at top and bottom by cardboard and glue

seat made from strips of wood with plywood back

wading pool made from plastic tray

wood frame containing sand

More ideas

Make a wading pool or a sandbox for your playground.

base of blockboard, particleboard, hardboard or plywood

Notes for parents and teachers

Further reading

WOOD WORKS
by William F. Brown
(Atheneum, 1984)

BALSA WOOD CRAFT
by Peter Weiss
(Lothrop, 1972)

WOODWORKING FOR KIDS
(Doubleday, 1978)

The projects suggested in this book are intended to provoke thought concerning design for woodwork. Children should be discouraged from making detailed copies of the examples given. Rather, we need to foster the sort of self-confidence that will enable children to make a more personal response. To this end, it is important to promote discussion at every stage of the project, encouraging children to think for themselves and use their imagination.

It is necessary to ensure that all tools remain in good working order. Badly maintained tools are a safety hazard and cause frustration. Vises should be cleaned with a brush, and tightening screws oiled occasionally. A lightly oiled cloth should be used to clean saws and to prevent the blades from rusting. The central spindle and gear wheel of hand drills should be oiled occasionally. Check that the handles of files are secure and that bench hooks (sawing boards) are not worn.

Children find bench hooks designed for adults difficult to hold while sawing. Smaller bench hooks are easy to make. For a left-handed child, the sawing gap needs to be positioned on the left-hand side of the bench hook.

Woodcraft tools are dangerous only if wrongly or carelessly used. It is important to teach the safe handling of tools and continue to stress the importance of safety matters. Where children are taught safe procedures, accidents should be rare. However, a first aid kit should be kept readily available and the contents replenished as necessary.

Glossary

All-purpose glue White, non-waterproof glue that is sold in plastic containers. This glue will attach wood to wood as well as wood to cardboard, cloth and paper.

Bit A hole-boring piece that fits into a drill. Bits are available in many sizes. Twist bits are needed for making holes through wood.

Collage A picture or design made from pieces of material that have been glued onto a background.

Hardwood The wood of deciduous trees, that is, trees that lose their leaves in autumn. Examples are ash, beech, elm and oak.

Pre-planed wood Wood that is smoothed, by planing, before it is sold.

Sandpaper Paper with a rough surface used to smooth wood.

Softwood The wood of coniferous trees, that is, trees with cones and needle-pointed leaves. They do not lose their leaves in autumn. Examples are cedar, fir, pine and spruce.

Veneer A paper-thin sheet of wood.

WOOD
Index